Three Littl

Story by June Melser and Joy Cowley • Illustrations by David Cowe

Crack. Crack. Crack.

One little duck,

two little ducks,

three little ducks
came out of the eggs.

Mother Duck
looked after them.

And, waddle, waddle, waddle,
they did.

"Come and swim,"
said Mother Duck.

And, paddle, paddle, paddle,
they did.

"Come and eat,"
said Mother Duck.

And, gobble, gobble, gobble,
they did.

"Come and sleep,"
said Mother Duck.

And, snuggle, snuggle, snuggle,
they did.

"Come and hide,"
said Mother Duck.

And, very, very quietly,
they did.

One day Mother Duck said,
"Come and fly."

And, flop, flop, flop,
they couldn't. Then...

flap, flap, flap,
they did.